"I Can Crochet"

For assistance in working the stitches, be sure to visit our exciting new Web site: StitchGuide.com. The basic stitches are shown using words, illustrations, and even a video of the actual stitch being worked!

Crochet is more than a hobby. It is an art form that has survived for thousands of years. Crochet has even been found in the tombs of ancient kings and queens.

With crochet, you can express your own style.

You can create things for yourself as well as gifts for all your family and friends.

Crochet also helps to develop hand and eye coordination and stimulates both the creative and logic thought processes in the brain.

Stuff You Need

Only a few things are needed to crochet, like yarn, a hook and a needle. Some you may need to buy and some you may already have at home.

Each pattern has a list of supplies and special tools needed to make the project, like how much of each color yarn you need and what size hook to use.

Crochet hooks come in a wide range of sizes. The sizes are marked on the hook as a letter or a number *(see photo 2)*. The best size to start with is a G hook. You will be using a G hook, an H hook and an I hook for the patterns in this book.

There are many types of yarn and they come in a special loosely-wrapped ball called a skein. You will be using worsted yarn for all of the projects in this book.

Skein wrappers have extra information about the yarn. The amount, color name, dye lot number, and care and washing instructions.

When you are picking the colors of yarn for your project, make sure all of the dye lot numbers written on the yarn label are the same *(see photo 3)*.

Some skeins are specially made so you do not have to rewind them into a ball like old-fashioned skeins.

First, take the outside strand *(see photo 4)* and

Pull this strand out of skein first

Pull this strand out of skein to crochet with

pull it out of the end it is tucked into. This end keeps the skein from coming loose until you are ready to use it. Now the center strand will come out easily.

A large tapestry needle is used for sewing crochet pieces together. This kind of needle has a large eye so thick yarn will fit through it.

There are needle threaders to help get the yarn through the eye of the needle. First, fit the curve at the end of the threader through the eye, then put the end of the yarn in the curve, and finally pull the yarn back through the eye with the threader *(see photo 5)*.

If you don't have a needle threader, fold a narrow strip of paper over the end of the yarn and push the paper through the eye.

You will need a pair of scissors to cut the yarn when you are finished.

Crochet patterns usually do not list things like scissors and needle threaders in the materials list. It is understood that you will always need them.

If you need a ruler to measure something, we have drawn one for you to use on the edge of this page.

Now you are ready to crochet!

What Is Crochet?

Basically crochet is making fabric with yarn by pulling one loop through another loop with a hook.

To Begin

A slip knot is the first thing you make in every crochet project. It attaches the yarn to the hook and makes your first loop.

Most patterns will not tell you to make a slip knot because it is done every time you start.

To make a slip knot:

Step 1: Make a loop in the yarn *(see photo 1).*

Strand coming from skein

Reach through the loop and pick up the strand coming from the skein

6 inch end

Step 2: Reach through the loop, pick up the strand *(see photo 1)*; holding both ends of the yarn, pull the strand through the loop *(see photo 2).*

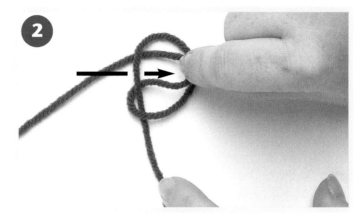

You now have a slip knot *(see photo 3).*

Slip knot

Step 3: Put the loop on the hook and pull the short end of the yarn just a little to tighten the knot *(see photo 4).*

If you pull too much, the slip knot will be too tight and it will be hard to adjust the size of the loop.

You can tell if the knot is tied right by pulling on the ends. When you pull the short end, the loop should get larger. When you pull the long end, the loop should get smaller.

You want the loop to be large enough so the end of the hook will go through it easily without getting caught.

Practice tying a slip knot before moving onto the next step.

There are several ways to hold the yarn and hook. Try each one and choose the way that feels the best to you.

To hold the hook and yarn:
Step 1: Hold the hook in one hand like a pencil *(see photo 5)* or like a knife *(see photo 6).*

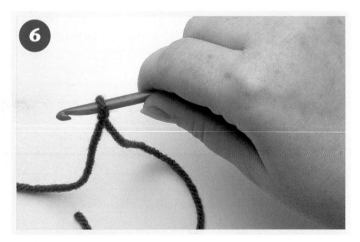

Step 2: Put the yarn in your other hand like you see it in photo 7, and pinch the slip knot with your middle finger and thumb like you see it in photo 8. This keeps the loop on the hook from spinning and sliding around while you crochet.

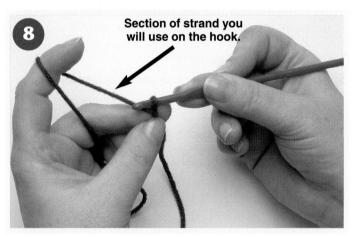

Section of strand you will use on the hook.

Practice holding the hook and yarn until it feels comfortable in your hands. The important thing is to hold the yarn in a way that feels right to you. Just make sure it wrapped over your index finger and you are able to hold the slip knot between the middle finger and thumb.

The yarn stretched between your index finger and the slip knot is the part you use to make stitches *(see photo 8).*

How tight you keep the yarn wrapped around the little finger controls how fast the yarn slides through your hand. If it is going faster than you want, you can weave it through several fingers to slow it down. ○

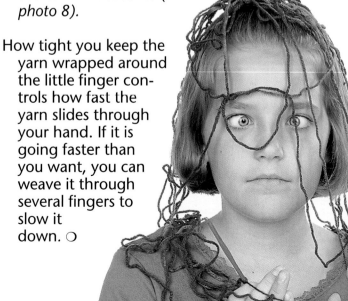

Chain Stitch Shoelaces – Lesson 2

In this pattern, you will learn to make a chain (ch) stitch. You will also learn to fasten off.

Materials:
- ○ Small amount of worsted yarn
- ○ Tapestry needle
- ○ G hook

Shoelace (make 2)

Make chains until your shoelace is 22 inches long or the length you want.

To make a chain stitch:

Step 1: Make a slip knot and put it on the hook.

Step 2: Wrap the yarn over the hook from **back to front** *(see photo 1).* This is called a <u>yarn</u> over (yo). This is what you do when you see the letters <u>yo</u> in a crochet pattern.

Step 3: Twist the hook so the front is facing down and pull the hook to the right so the yarn-over goes through the loop on the hook and the loop on the hook slides off.

The first chain is done and a new loop is on the hook (see photo 2).

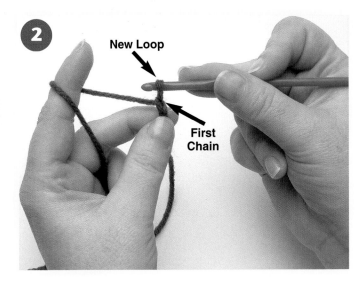

2 **New Loop** **First Chain**

For each chain, yarn over and pull it through the loop on the hook.

Remember to pinch the chain just below the hook every few stitches to keep them below the hook *(see photo 3).* If you let go of the

1 **Wrap yarn over front of hook.**

3

chain, you will lose control and the loop will spin and slide around on the hook.

Continue making chains. When your shoelace is long enough, you are ready to cut and hide the yarn end. This is called <u>fasten off</u>.

To fasten off:
Step 1: Cut the yarn about 6 inches past the loop on the hook. Yarn over with the 6-inch end and pull the end all the way through the loop *(see illustration 1)*.

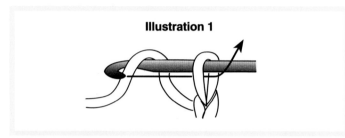

Illustration 1

Step 2: To hide the end of the yarn, thread it through the tapestry needle and weave the thread through the back of the stitches *(see illustration 2)*.

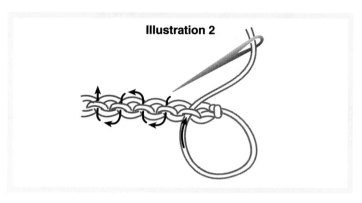

Illustration 2

When you see the letters <u>ch</u> in a crochet pattern, you make a chain stitch. Sometimes there will be a number in front of these letters. This number tells you how many chains to make. ○

Wow! I can watch stitches being made on Stitchguide.com!

Single Crochet Scrunchie – Lesson 3

In this pattern, you will learn to make a single crochet (sc) stitch worked around a ring. You will also be making a chain (ch) stitch from lesson 2.

Materials:
- ❍ 1 oz. worsted yarn
- ❍ Elastic ponytail band
- ❍ G hook

Scrunchie
Make a single crochet around the elastic band.

To make a single crochet around a ring:
Step 1: Put a slip knot on the hook and hold it above the ring *(see photo 1)*.

Step 2: Insert the hook through the ring, yarn over *(see photo 2)* and pull it back through the ring.

You now have 2 loops on the hook *(see photo 3)*.

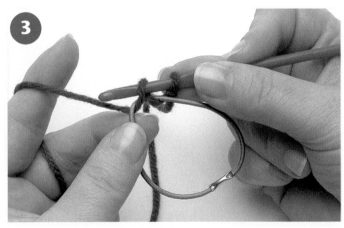

Step 3: Yarn over again and pull the yarn through both loops on the hook *(see arrow on photo 4)*.

The first single crochet is done and a new loop is on the hook (see photo 5).

Now make 20 chains. For the next single crochet, repeat steps two and three *(see photo 6).*

Keep making chain-20 loops and single crochet stitches around the ring until the elastic band is covered.

When you have made all the loops you want for your Scrunchie, you are ready to fasten off *(see lesson 2 on page 6).*

When you see the letters <u>sc</u> in a crochet pattern, you make a single crochet. Sometimes there will be a number in front of these letters. This tells you how many stitches on the last row or round to work into. ○

I've got the crochet world by the tail!

Half Double Crochet
Friendship Bracelets – Lesson 4

In this pattern, you will learn to make a regular single crochet (sc) stitch and a half double crochet (hdc) stitch. You will also be making a chain (ch) stitch from lesson 2.

You will also learn to work in turned rows, learn to use repeating symbols and learn to crochet with beads.

Crochet can be decorated with beads and buttons, as well as many other items. They can be added to the yarn and pulled into place as you work or sew them on the finished piece with a needle and thread.

Materials:
- ○ 1 oz. worsted yarn
- ○ 10 pony beads
- ○ Tapestry needle
- ○ G hook

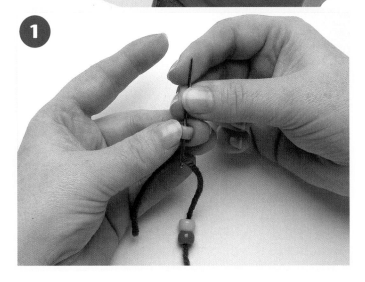

Bracelet
Row 1:
Thread the yarn on the tapestry needle and string ten beads onto the yarn *(see photo 1).*

Take the needle off the yarn. These beads will be pushed along the yarn until they are needed in the pattern. Make 34 chains.

This strand of chain stitches is called a <u>starting chain</u> and it is used as the foundation for your first row of stitches.

Make a single crochet in the second chain from the hook *(see photo 2).*

Second chain from hook

Next, make a single crochet in each chain across to the end *(see photo 3).*

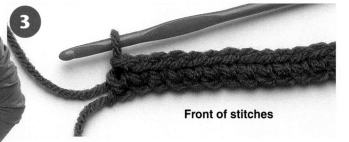

Front of stitches

Now you are ready to <u>turn</u>. This changes the direction of the first row so you can work the new row from right to left.

To turn:
Flip the row of stitches over so the back of the stitches are facing you *(see photo 4).*

Back of stitches

Row 2: Make 2 chains *(see photo 5)*.

This first strand of chain stitches is called a <u>turning chain</u>.

The turning chain is used and counted as a regular stitch unless the instructions tell you not to use it.

Make a half double crochet in the next stitch on the last row.

To make a half double crochet:
Step 1: Yarn over *(see photo 6),* and insert the

hook through the top loops of the next stitch *(see photo 7)*.

Step 2: Yarn over again and pull through the stitch *(see photo 8);* you have 3 loops on the hook.

Step 3: Yarn over and pull through all 3 loops on the hook at the same time.

The first half double crochet is done and a new loop is on the hook (see photo 9).

Make a hdc in the next stitch on the last row.

*Pull a bead on the yarn up next to the stitch just made *(see photo 10),* make one chain, skip the

next stitch on the last row, make a half double crochet in the next 2 stitches *(see photo 11);* repeat from the * 9 more times.

11

To repeat from a * symbol:

Go back to the * and work all of the instructions again until you reach the word "repeat". In this pattern, you will repeat the instructions the number of times after the second * symbol.

After all of the repeats are done, turn.

Row 3: Make one chain, make a single crochet in each stitch and in each chain across row 2, **do not turn.**

You will be making the next part in the ends of the rows.

To work in the end of a row:

As you make a stitch, you insert the hook through loops on the side of the last stitch in the row.

For the **first tie,** make one chain, insert the hook in the end of row 3, yarn over and pull through, (insert the hook in the end of the next row, yarn over and pull through) 2 times *(see photo 12).*

12

When there is a set of parenthesis ( ) symbols or bracket [ ] symbols, you will repeat only the instructions between the symbols.

When there is a number of times after the second

symbol, you will repeat the instructions that many times.

You should have 4 loops on the hook, yarn over and pull through all 4 loops *(see photo 13),*

13

make 15 chains *(see photo 14).* Fasten off.

14

For the **second tie,** make a slip knot and put it on the hook, insert the hook in the other end of row 1, yarn over and pull through, (insert the hook in the end of the next row, yarn over and pull through) 2 times; yarn over and pull through all 4 loops, make 15 chains. Fasten off. ○

My friends are going to love these!

Double Crochet Scarf - Lesson 5

In this pattern, you will learn to make a double crochet (dc) stitch. You will also be making a chain (ch) stitch from lesson 2.

You will be working turned rows and you will also learn to make Fringe.

Materials:
- ○ 3½ oz. worsted yarn
- ○ G hook

Scarf
Row 1: Make 23 chains, make a double crochet in the fourth chain from the hook.

To make a double crochet:
Step 1: Yarn over and insert the hook in the stitch *(see photo 1).*

Step 2: Yarn over again and pull through the stitch, you have 3 loops on the hook *(see photo 2).*

Step 3: Yarn over and pull through 2 loops on the hook *(see photo 3).*

Step 4: Yarn over again and pull through last 2 loops on the hook.

The first double crochet is done and a new loop is on the hook (see photo 4).

Make a double crochet in each remaining chain of the starting chain, turn.

Row 2: Make 3 chains *(see photo 5).*

Remember, this strand of chains is called a turning chain and they count the same as a double crochet stitch.

Make a double crochet in the next two stitches on the last row, (make one chain, skip the next stitch on the last row, make a double crochet in the next stitch) 8 times, make a double crochet in the next stitch, make the last double crochet in the top of the turning chain at the end of row 1 *(see photo 6),* turn.

Remember, the turning chain is used just like a stitch unless the pattern says to do something else.

Row 3: Make 3 chains, make a double crochet in the next 2 stitches on the last row,

(make one chain, skip next the chain on the last row, make a double crochet in the next stitch—*see photo 7*) 8 times, make a double crochet in the last two stitches, turn.

Rows 4-66: Repeat row 3 over and over until you have 66 rows or make it as long as you want. **Before making it really long,** make sure you have enough extra yarn for the additional length.

Row 67: Make 3 chains, make a double crochet in each stitch and in each chain across to end. Fasten off.

Fringe
Make a 7-inch fringe in each stitch across each short end of the Scarf.

To make a fringe:
Step 1: Cut a piece from the skein of yarn 14 inches long. Fold the piece of yarn in half *(see illustration A).*

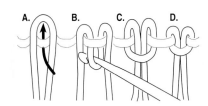

Step 2: Insert the hook through a stitch or space, catch the folded end with the hook and pull the folded end of the yarn back through *(see illustration B).*

Step 3: Insert the hook through the folded end, catch the ends of the yarn with the hook and pull them back through the fold *(see illustration C).*

Step 4: Pull on the ends to tighten the fringe in place *(see illustration D).*

When all of the Fringe are done, trim the ends to make them even. ○

Purse With Slip Stitch Strap – Lesson 6

In this pattern, you will learn to make a slip stitch (sl st). You will also be making a chain (ch) stitch from lesson 2, a single crochet (sc) stitch from lesson 3 and a half double crochet (hdc) stitch from lesson 4.

You will be working turned rows. You will also learn to join with a single crochet, learn to crochet pieces together and learn to make a Tassel.

Materials:
- ○ Worsted yarn:
    - 2 oz. multicolored yarn
    - 1 oz. solid color yarn
- ○ ⅞" button
- ○ 4" square piece of cardboard
- ○ Sewing thread to match button
- ○ Tapestry needle and sewing needle
- ○ G hook

Sides and Flap
Row 1: Using the multicolored yarn, make 26 chains, make a half double crochet in the third chain from the hook *(see photo 1)*; make a half double crochet in each chain across, turn.

Row 2: Make 2 chains *(this is your turning chain and it is used just like the turning chain we made in lesson 4)*, make a half double crochet in each stitch across, turn.

Rows 3-35: Repeat row 2 over and over until you have 35 rows or as many rows as you need to make it about 10½ inches long. At the end of the last row, fasten off.

Folding
Fold the sides and flap piece placing rows 1-14 over rows 16-29. Pin the two layers together with the tapestry needle to hold them together while making the outer edge.

Outer Edge
Hold the folded crochet piece with the back side and the flap facing you.

Starting in the ends of the rows next to the fold, join the multicolored yarn with a single crochet.

To join with a single crochet:
Step 1: Using the multicolored yarn make a slip knot and put it on the hook.

Step 2: Insert the hook through both edges at the same time *(see photo 2)*, yarn over and pull through the ends of the rows.

Step 3: Yarn over again and pull through both loops on the hook *(see photo 3).*

Evenly space single crochet stitches across to the last row on the flap *(see photo 4).*

Too many stitches worked across the edge will make it ruffle *(see photo 5).*

Not enough stitches will make it curl up *(see photo 6).*

Next, make a single crochet in each of the first 11 stitches on the last row of the flap.

For the button loop, make 7 chains, skip the next 3 stitches on the last row, make a single crochet in each of the last 11 stitches.

Now you are ready to work in the ends of the rows across the other edge of the folded piece.

Working the same way you did on the first edge, evenly space single crochet stitches across to the fold. Fasten off.

Slip Stitch Strap
Row 1: Hold the purse with the front side facing you, join the multicolored yarn with a single crochet in the first stitch worked into the end of row 1 *(see photo 7).*

Make a single crochet in the next 2 stitches.

Next, make chains until the piece is 33 inches long or the length you want for your strap.

To connect the end of the strap, go over to the opposite end of row 1 *(see photo 8).*

Make a single crochet in the 3 stitches worked into the end of the rows, turn *(see photo 9).*

Row 2: Slip stitch in the first stitch.

To make a slip stitch:
Step 1: Insert the hook through the top of the next stitch.

Step 2: Yarn over and pull through the stitch and the loop on the hook.

The first slip stitch is done and a new loop is on the hook.

Make a slip stitch in the next 2 stitch-es, make a slip stitch in each

chain *(see photo 10)* across to the first 3 single crochet on row 1, make a slip stitch in each of the 3 stitches. Fasten off.

Thread the sewing needle with the sewing thread. Sew the button to the center front of the purse about one inch below the edge.

Tassel (make 2)

To make a Tassel:
Step 1: Wind the solid yarn around the cardboard about 25 times *(see illustration A).*

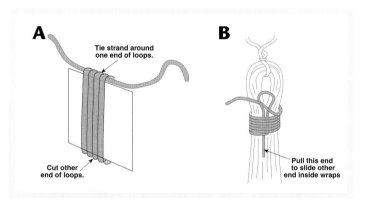

Step 2: Tie an 8 inch piece of the solid yarn tightly around one end of all the loops *(see illustration A).* Cut the other end of all the loops.

Step 3: Cut a 12 inch piece of solid yarn. Making a loop at the top, wrap the yarn tightly several times around all of the strands about one half inch from the top *(see illustration B).*

Step 4: Insert the loose end of the 12-inch piece through the loop and pull the other end so the loop slides down inside the wraps. Cut off the excess end.

Using the ends of the 8 inch tie, sew the Tassels to each bottom corner of the purse as shown in the photo. ○

Granny Square Vest – Lesson 7

In this pattern, you will learn to work in joined rounds. You will also learn to change the gauge of the stitches to make an item larger or smaller and learn to sew crochet pieces together.

You will be making a chain (ch) stitch from lesson 2, a single crochet (sc) stitch from lesson 3, a double crochet (dc) stitch from lesson 5 and a slip stitch (sl st) from lesson 6.

Finished Sizes:

Instructions will make a girl's small (26-27" chest), medium (28-29" chest) and large (30-31" chest).

Materials:

○ Worsted yarn (the amounts listed below will make up to the large size; when making a project larger than the pattern states, always buy extra yarn):

   2 oz. solid color yarn for round 1
   3 oz. multicolored yarn for round 2
   4 oz. solid color yarn for round 3

○ 7" square piece of cardboard
○ Tapestry needle
○ G hook for small size
○ H hook for medium size
○ I hook for large size

Now it's time to visit my granny.

For crochet that has to be a certain size to fit, such as clothing, the gauge is important.

In crochet, <u>gauge</u> is how wide and how tall a stitch is. The size you make the stitches will affect the finished size of the piece.

When you need to make a stitch larger or smaller, you can change the size by using a different size hook.

In this pattern we will change the size of the square to make three different sizes.

Gauge:

For the small size vest, use a G hook to make 3½" squares.

For the medium size vest, use an H hook to make 3¾" squares.

For the large size vest, use an I hook to make 4" squares (*see illustrations on next page*).

sew the squares together from corner to corner (*see photo 5*).

All the edges will be sewn together through the back loops.

Keep sewing squares end to end until you have a strip with eight squares.

Now make another strip the same as the first one. Make two more strips with three squares in each strip.

Arrange the strips as shown in illustration B and sew the edges of the strips together where they meet.

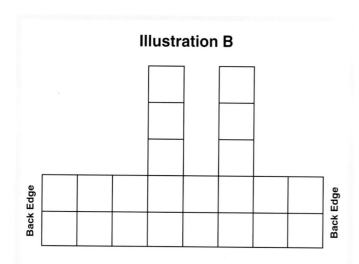

Illustration B

Sew the ends of the long strips together for the back seam.

Sew the end of each shoulder strip to the edge of the squares as shown in illustration C.

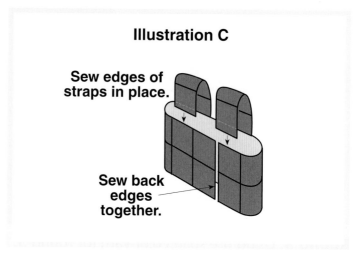

Illustration C

Sew edges of straps in place.

Sew back edges together.

Fringe
Working in the chain spaces around the bottom edge of the vest, make two 6-inch fringe evenly spaced apart on each square.

To make a multi-strand fringe:
Step 1: Wrap the yarn around the cardboard square six times. Cut one end of all the loops on the cardboard. This makes all the strands at the same time.

Step 2: Hold all the strands of yarn made in step 1 together and fold them in half. Insert the hook through a stitch or space, catch the folded end with the hook and pull the folded end of all the strands back through.

Step 3: Reach through the folded end and pull the ends of the yarn back through the fold.

Step 4: Pull the ends to tighten the fringe in place.

When all of the Fringe are done, trim the ends to make them even. ○

Striped Afghan – Lesson 8

In this pattern you will learn to crochet with two strands of yarn at the same time and learn to work on the opposite side of the starting chain.

You will be working turned rows.

You will be making a chain (ch) stitch from lesson 2, a single crochet (sc) stitch from lesson 3 and a double crochet (dc) stitch from lesson 5.

You can change the size of this lapghan by using a larger hook or by adding extra chains to the starting chain and by working more rows. Remember, when making a project larger than the pattern states, always buy extra yarn.

Materials:
- ○ Worsted yarn:
  - 12 oz. of multicolored yarn
  - 12 oz. purple
  - 10 oz. teal
  - 8 oz. white
- ○ 9" square piece of cardboard
- ○ Tapestry needle
- ○ H hook

An afghan just my size!

Afghan

Row 1: Hold 2 strands of purple yarn together as one *(see photo 1)*, make 72 chains, make a double crochet in the fourth chain from the hook, make a double crochet in each chain across, turn.

Row 2: Make 4 chains; these 4 chains will count as the first double crochet and the first chain space.

Skip the next stitch on the last row, make a double crochet in the next stitch.

(Make one chain, skip the next stitch, make a double crochet in the next stitch) across.

When the word "across" or "around" appears after a set of parentheses ( ) or brackets [ ], this means that the repeat will work evenly across and you will repeat the instructions inside the symbols over and over until you reach the end of the row or round.

When all of the repeats have been worked, turn.

Row 3: Make 3 chains, make a double crochet in the first chain space on the last row.

To work in a space:

As you make a stitch, insert the hook through the opening below the chain instead of through the loops of the chain *(see photo 2).*

Make a double crochet in each stitch and in each chain space across the last row.

Remember that the turning chain is treated the same as the other stitches and chain spaces of the row.

Make a double crochet in the chain space and make a double crochet in the top of the remaining three chains.

At the end of this row, fasten off. Do not turn at the end of row 3.

Row 4: Hold 2 strands of white together as one

and join the yarn in the first stitch of the last row with a single crochet *(see lesson 6).* Make a single crochet in each stitch across the last row. Fasten off. Do not turn at the end of row 4.

Row 5: Hold 2 strands of multicolored together as one and join the yarn in the first stitch of the last row with a single crochet, make 2 chains *(see photo 3).*

The single crochet and the 2 chains make a different type of turning chain. It counts as a double crochet just like the turning chain-3 you learned in Lesson 5. This kind of turning chain looks more like a regular double crochet.

Make a double crochet in each stitch across last row, turn.

Row 6: Make 4 chains, skip the next stitch on last row, make a double crochet in the next stitch, (make one chain, skip the next stitch on last row, make a double crochet in the next st) across, turn.

Row 7: Make 3 chains, make a double crochet in each chain space and a double crochet in each stitch across last row. Fasten off. **Do not turn.**

Row 8: Hold 2 strands of white yarn together as one and join in the first stitch of the last row with a single crochet, make a single crochet in each stitch across the last row. Fasten off. **Do not turn.**

Row 9: Hold 2 strands of teal together as one and join in the first stitch of the last row with a single crochet, make 2 chains, make a double crochet in each stitch across the last row, turn.

Row 10: Make 4 chains, skip the next stitch on the last row, make a double crochet in the next stitch, (make one chain, skip the next stitch on last row, make a double crochet in the next st) across, turn.

Row 11: Make 3 chains, make a double crochet in each chain space and a double crochet in each stitch across the last row. Fasten off. **Do not turn.**

In the following rows, you will be using the instructions for rows 4 through 11 over and over. But you will change the colors of yarn for some of the rows to make the different color stripes (see photo 4).

Rows 12-16: Repeat rows 4 through 8.

Rows 17-19: Using purple yarn, repeat rows 9 through 11.

Rows 20-24: Repeat rows 4 through 8 again.

Rows 25-27: Using teal yarn, repeat rows 9 through 11.

Rows 28-32: Repeat rows 4 through 8.

Rows 33-35: Using purple yarn, repeat rows 9 through 11.

Rows 36-40: Repeat rows 4 through 8 again.

Rows 41-43: Using teal yarn, repeat rows 9 through 11.

Rows 44-48: Repeat rows 4 through 8.

Rows 49-51: Using purple yarn, repeat rows 9 through 11.

Row 52: Hold 2 strands of white together as one and join in the first stitch of the last row with a single crochet, (make 3 chains, skip the next st on the last row, make a single crochet in the next stitch) across. Fasten off. **Do not turn.**

Row 53: Working in the opposite side of the starting chain,

To work in opposite side of the starting chain:
Step 1: Turn the lapghan so that row 1 is upside down.

Step 2: As you make the first st, insert the hook through the remaining loop of the chains already worked into *(see photo 5).*

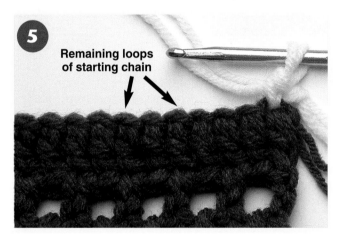

Remaining loops of starting chain

Hold 2 strands of white together as one and join in the first stitch of the last row with a single crochet *(see photo 5),* (make 3 chains, skip the next st on the last row, make a single crochet in the next stitch) across. Fasten off.

Fringe
Using purple yarn and the 9"-square piece of cardboard, make a fringe *(see instructions for multi-strand fringe on page 18)* in each chain-3 space across each end of lapghan. ○

Continuous Rounds Hat – Lesson 9

In this pattern, you will learn to work in continuous rounds. You also will learn about increasing and about stitch counts. You will also learn how to make reverse sc for a decorative edging.

You will be making a chain (ch) stitch from lesson 2, a single crochet (sc) stitch from lesson 3 and a slip stitch from lesson 6.

Finished Size:
Hat will fit up to a 21-inch head.

Materials:
○ 3 oz. solid color worsted yarn
○ Stitch markers (see below)
○ G hook

<u>Continuous rounds</u> in crochet are worked around and around without joining with a slip stitch as in joined rounds *(see lesson 7 on page 19).*

When working in continuous rounds that have increases or decreases, it is important to keep up with the first stitch of each round so you can make the right number of stitches.

To do this you place a marker in the stitch when it is done.

Several things can be used to <u>mark stitches</u>. Bobby pins, knit stitch markers and even a piece of yarn that is a different color.

When the first stitch of each new round is made, the marker is taken out of the last round and moved to the new round.

Sometimes you will want to leave the markers in place for several rounds at a time in case it is a lengthy or detailed pattern.

Hat
Round 1: With purple yarn, make 4 chains, make a slip stitch in the first chain of the chain-4 to form a crochet ring *(see lesson 7).*

Make a single crochet in the ring *(see lesson 3),* place a marker in this stitch.

Make 7 more single crochet in the ring, do not join the first and last

stitch of the rounds unless the instructions tell you to. (8 single crochet made) *(see photo 1)*

In some crochet patterns it is important to have the correct number of stitches in each row or round.

The number inside a set of parentheses ( ) at the end of a row or round is called a <u>stitch count</u>.

This is a reminder to make sure you have the right amount of stitches so the next round you make will be right.

Round 2: Make 2 single crochet in the marked first stitch.

Whenever you make more than one stitch into a stitch, it is called an <u>increase</u> (inc). This is done to make a piece larger or to add shaping to a piece.

Make 2 single crochet in each stitch around. *(16 single crochet made) (see photo 2)*

Rounds 3-4: Make a single crochet in the first stitch and move the marker to the stitch just made.

Be sure to move the marker to the first stitch of each new round you make. (see photo 3)

Make 2 single crochet in the next stitch.

(Make a single crochet in the next stitch, make 2 single crochet in the next stitch) 7 times. *(24 single crochet made on round 3; 36 single crochet made on round 4)*

Round 5: Make a single crochet in each stitch around.

Round 6: (Make a single crochet in the next 3 stitches, make 2 single crochet in the next stitch) 8 times. *(45 single crochet)*

Round 7: Make a single crochet in each stitch around.

Round 8: Make a single crochet in the first stitch, (make a single crochet in the next 3 stitches, make 2 single crochet in the next stitch) 11 times. *(56 single crochet)*

Round 9: Make a single crochet in each stitch around.

Round 10: Make a single crochet in the first stitch, (make a single crochet in the next 4 stitches, make 2 single crochet in the next stitch) 11 times. *(67 single crochet)*

Rounds 11-12: Make a single crochet in each stitch around.

Round 13: Make a single crochet in the first stitch, (make a single crochet in the next 5 stitches, make 2 single crochet in the next stitch) 11 times. *(78 single crochet)*

Rounds 14-16: Make a single crochet in each stitch around.

Round 17: Make a single crochet in the first stitch, (make a single crochet in the next six stitches, make 2 single crochet in the next stitch) 11 times. *(89 single crochet)*

Rounds 18-35: Make a single crochet in each stitch around.

At the end of the last round, join with a slip stitch in the marked single crochet made for that round.

Round 36: Make one chain; working from left to right, <u>reverse single crochet</u> in each stitch around,

To make reverse single crochet:
For regular crochet, you work in a right-to-left direction. For reverse single crochet you work in the opposite direction which gives this decorative edging stitch a twisted rope look.

Step 1: Insert the hook through the stitch to the

right of the turning chain one *(see photos 4 and 5),*

yarn over and pull through *(see photo 6).* This loop should be loose enough to come up and cross over the turning chain.

Step 2: Yarn over again and pull through both loops on the hook *(see photo 7).*

The first reverse single crochet is done and a new loop is on the hook (see photo 8).

Step 3: For the next reverse single crochet, insert the hook through the next stitch to the right of the last reverse single crochet made *(see photo 8).*

Step 4: Yarn over and pull through *(see photo 9),* remember to pull this loop up so it is loose enough to cross over the front of the last stitch.

Step 5: Yarn over again and pull through both loops on the hook.

Continue repeating steps 3-5 until you get back to the turning chain one. Join with a slip stitch at the base of the first reverse single crochet made. Fasten off.

Finishing
You can add additional decoration by making a Scrunchie *(see lesson 3)* or Daisies *(see lesson 10).*

Sewing on large colorful buttons can create a different look for your hat.

Try making the last round of reverse single crochet in a different color. ○

Treble Crochet Daisy Accent – Lesson 10

In this pattern, you will learn to make a treble crochet (tr) stitch.

You will be working in joined rounds.

You will also be making a chain (ch) stitch from lesson 2, a single crochet (sc) stitch from lesson 3, a half double crochet (hdc) stitch from lesson 4 and a slip stitch from lesson 6.

Finished Sizes:
About 3 inches across the middle of the Small Daisy.
About 4½" across the middle of the Large daisy.

Materials for each Small Daisy:
❍ Worsted yarn:
    Small amount (about 10 yards) of white
    Small amount (about 5 yards) of yellow
❍ G hook

Materials for each Large Daisy:
❍ Worsted yarn:
    Small amount (about 20 yards)
     of white
    Small amount (about 10 yards)
     of yellow
❍ H hook

Small Daisy
Round 1: With G hook and yellow yarn, make 4 chains, slip stitch in the first chain to form a crochet ring, make 3 chains *(this counts as the first double crochet)*, make 15 half double crochet in the ring. *(See photo 1)*

Join with a slip stitch *(see Lesson 7)* in the top of the chain-3 at the beginning of the round. Fasten off. *(16 half double crochet made)*

Round 2: Join the white yarn with a slip stitch in any stitch on the last round.

Now you are ready to make a petal. You will make all of the following stitches into the same stitch.

Make a single crochet in the next stitch, make 3
chains, *(see photo 2)*

insert the hook in the same stitch as the single
crochet to make a treble crochet.

To make a treble crochet stitch:

Step 1: Yarn over 2 times *(see photo 3)*, insert the
hook in the stitch.

Step 2: Yarn over again and pull through *(see
photo 4)*, you will have 4 loops on the hook.

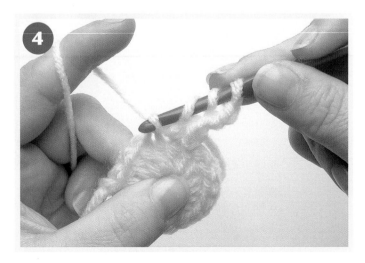

Step 3: (Yarn over and pull through 2 loops on
the hook) 3 times *(see photos 5-7)*.

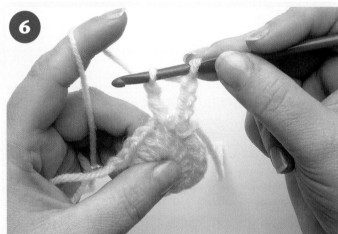

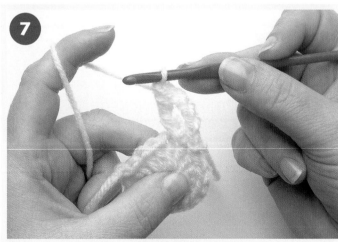

*The treble crochet is done and a new loop is on
the hook.*

Make 3 chains, make a single crochet in the same
stitch as the treble crochet; the first petal is
done. *(See photo 8)*

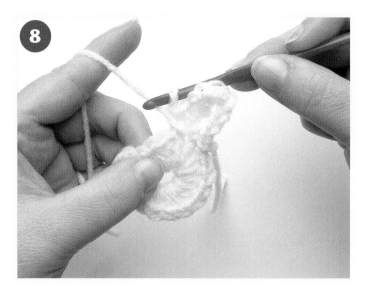

8

The Small Daisy can be used to decorate picture frames, clothing, hats, belts and hair clips. You can even sew them on jeans as a decorative patch to cover a small tear or spot!

The Large Daisy can be used as a coaster, a wall decal, a binder decal, backpack patch or a package decoration instead of a bow.

These Daisies can be sewn or glued to almost anything you want to put them on. ○

Oops-a-daisy, I've been framed!

Step 4: Slip stitch in the next stitch.

Step 5: For the next petal, make (a single crochet, 3 chains, a treble crochet, 3 more chains, and one more single crochet) in the next stitch; the second petal is done. *(See photo 9)*

9

Repeat steps 4 and 5 to make 6 more petals.

Join with a slip stitch in the first slip stitch at the beginning of the round. Fasten off.

Large Daisy
Using an H hook and 2 strands of yarn held together as you work *(see lesson 8)*, repeat the instructions for the small daisy.

Stitch Guide
for left-handed stitchers

STANDARD ABBREVIATIONS

beg ....beginning
ch, chs.................chain, chains
dc ....double crochet
dec ....decrease
hdc ....half double crochet
inc ....increase
lp, lps ....loop, loops
rnd, rnds ....round, rounds
sc...........................single crochet
sl st ....slip stitch
sp, sps ....space, spaces
st, sts ....stitch, stitches
tog ....together
tr ....treble crochet
yo ....yarn over

sc next 2 sts tog......(insert hook in next st, yo, pull through st) 2 times, yo, pull through all 3 lps on hook.

hdc next 2 sts tog.....(yo, insert hook in next st, yo, pull through st) 2 times, yo, pull through all 5 lps on hook.

dc next 2 sts tog......(yo, insert hook in next st, yo, pull through st, yo, pull through 2 lps on hook) 2 times, yo, pull through all 3 lps on hook.

Front post stitch—fp: Back post stitch—bp: When working post st, insert hook from left to right around post of st on previous row.

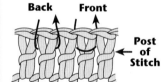

Chain—ch: Yo, pull through lp on hook.

Slip stitch—sl st: Insert hook in st, yo, pull through both lps on hook.

Single crochet—sc: Insert hook in st, yo, pull through st, yo, pull through both lps on hook.

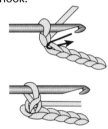

Front loop—front lp: Back loop—back lp:

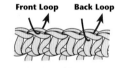

Change colors: Drop first color; with second color, pull through last 2 lps of st.

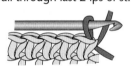

Half double crochet— hdc: Yo, insert hook in st, yo, pull through st, yo, pull through all 3 lps on hook.

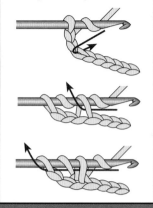

Double crochet—dc: Yo, insert hook in st, yo, pull through st, (yo, pull through 2 lps) 2 times.

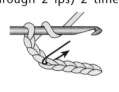
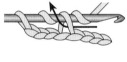
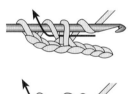
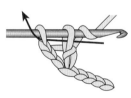

Treble crochet—tr: Yo 2 times, insert hook in st, yo, pull through st, (yo, pull through 2 lps) 3 times.

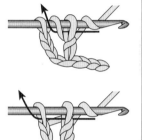

Double treble crochet— dtr: Yo 3 times, insert hook in st, yo, pull through st, (yo, pull through 2 lps) 4 times.

Now that you know how to crochet, you can put the knowledge to use by making crochet donations to charity. We have listed four of the most well-known charities so that you can visit their Web sites, or write for information.

Crochet a blanket to be given to a seriously ill or traumatized child or young adult:
Project Linus
P. O. Box 5621
Bloomington, IL 61702-5621
projectlinus.org

Crochet items for preemies, such as hats, booties, blankets and gowns:
TLC for Angels
850 Fort Plains Road
Howell, NJ 07731-1190
tlcforangels.tripod.com

Crochet 7" x 9" squares to be put together to make an afghan. It's all about keeping people warm!
Warm Up America!
2500 Lowell Road
Gastonia, NC 28054
craftyarncouncil.com/warmup.html

Provide needy children with cozy hats to keep them warm.
Caps for Kids--CYCA
c/o Bonnie Greene
30113 Echo Blue Drive
Penn Valley, CA 95946-9422
craftyarncouncil.com/caps.html

Stitch Guide
for right-handed stitchers

STANDARD ABBREVIATIONS

beg ....beginning
ch, chs.................chain, chains
dc ....double crochet
dec ....decrease
hdc ....half double crochet
inc ....increase
lp, lps.....................loop, loops
rnd, rnds ....round, rounds
sc.....................single crochet
sl st ....slip stitch
sp, sps ....space, spaces
st, sts.................stitch, stitches
tog ....together
tr ....treble crochet
yo ....yarn over

sc next 2 sts tog......(insert hook in next st, yo, pull through st) 2 times, yo, pull through all 3 lps on hook.

hdc next 2 sts tog.....(yo, insert hook in next st, yo, pull through st) 2 times, yo, pull through all 5 lps on hook.

dc next 2 sts tog......(yo, insert hook in next st, yo, pull through st, yo, pull through 2 lps on hook) 2 times, yo, pull through all 3 lps on hook.

Front post stitch—fp:
Back post stitch—bp: When working post st, insert hook from right to left around post of st on previous row.

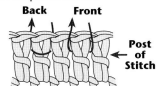

Chain—ch: Yo, pull through lp on hook.

Slip stitch—sl st: Insert hook in st, yo, pull through both lps on hook.

Single crochet—sc: Insert hook in st, yo, pull through st, yo, pull through both lps on hook.

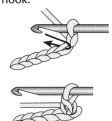

Front loop—front lp:
Back loop—back lp:

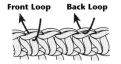

Change colors: Drop first color; with second color, pull through last 2 lps of st.

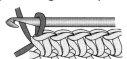

Half double crochet—hdc: Yo, insert hook in st, yo, pull through st, yo, pull through all 3 lps on hook.

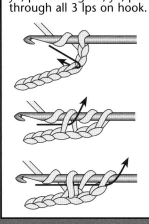

Double crochet—dc: Yo, insert hook in st, yo, pull through st, (yo, pull through 2 lps) 2 times.

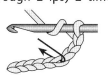

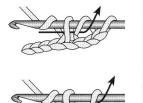

Treble crochet—tr: Yo 2 times, insert hook in st, yo, pull through st, (yo, pull through 2 lps) 3 times.

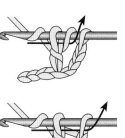

Double treble crochet—dtr: Yo 3 times, insert hook in st, yo, pull through st, (yo, pull through 2 lps) 4 times.

The patterns in this book are written using American crochet stitch terminology.
For our international customers, hook sizes, stitches and yarn definitions should be converted as follows:

But, as with all patterns, test your gauge (tension) to be sure.

US	=	UK
sl st (slip stitch)	=	sc (single crochet)
sc (single crochet)	=	dc (double crochet)
hdc (half double crochet)	=	htr (half treble crochet)
dc (double crochet)	=	tr (treble crochet)
tr (treble crochet)	=	dtr (double treble crochet)
dtr (double treble crochet)	=	ttr (triple treble crochet)
skip	=	miss

THREAD/YARNS

Bedspread Weight	=	No. 10 Cotton or Virtuoso
Sport Weight	=	4 Ply or thin DK
Worsted Weight	=	Thick DK or Aran

MEASUREMENTS

1"	=	2.54 cm
1 yd.	=	.9144 m
1 oz.	=	28.35 g

CROCHET HOOKS

Metric	US	Metric	US
.60mm	14	3.00mm	D/3
.75mm	12	3.50mm	E/4
1.00mm	10	4.00mm	F/5
1.50mm	6	4.50mm	G/6
1.75mm	5	5.00mm	H/8
2.00mm	B/1	5.50mm	I/9
2.50mm	C/2	6.00mm	J/10

PRODUCT DEVELOPMENT DIRECTOR—Andy Ashley / **PUBLISHING SERVICES DIRECTOR**—Ange Van Arman
CROCHET DESIGN MANAGER—Deborah Levy-Hamburg / **PRODUCT DEVELOPMENT STAFF**—Mickie Akins,
Darla Hassell, Sandra Miller Maxfield, Alice Mitchell, Elizabeth Ann White
SENIOR EDITOR—Donna Scott / **PROJECT EDITOR**—Liz Field
CROCHET EDITORIAL STAFF—Nina Marsh, Sharon Lothrop, Lyne Pickens, Shirley Brown
PHOTOGRAPHY STAFF—Scott Campbell, Andy J. Burnfield, Martha Coquat
PRODUCTION SUPERVISOR—Minette Smith / **COVER DESIGN**—Greg Smith / **GRAPHIC ARTISTS**—Cherie Pendley, Minette Smith
PRODUCTION COORDINATOR—Glenda Chamberlain

© 2001 Annie's Attic, LLC   All rights reserved.
1 Annie Lane, Big Sandy, Texas 75755 — AnniesAttic.com
Call 1 (800) LV-ANNIE for a free catalog — Call 1 (903) 636-4357 for Pattern Services
Every effort has been made to ensure that these instructions are accurate and complete.
We cannot, however, take responsibility for human error, typographical mistakes or variations in individual work.

ISBN: 978-1-59635-134-9

Printed in USA